Life Is Short, So Live It Now

101 Insights for Living Your Best Life

by **Steve Beck, CSP**

Praise for Steve Beck and "The Beck Effect"

"Steve, I still listen to your Great Day Every Day audio every day. It's worked wonders, not just for me by for my family, co-workers, and the quest. I'm inspired to live every day to the fullest, and I DO have a Great Day Every Day! The day I spent in your seminar has turned my life around."
Barb, Billings, MT

"Best seminar I've ever attended, hands down."
Deborah, Phoenix, AZ

"Mr. Beck: From the first seminar of yours I attended, you struck a chord in me that influenced by way of thinking and would bring me to believe in myself more than ever. The ideas you shared helped me construct a new foundation in my mind for what I want to accomplish, and helped pave the path that will eventually get me there. I keep repeating my daily affirmations – every day – and life is great."
Maureen, Glen Ellyn, IL

"Steve, thank you. I believe what I took away from your seminar will change my life."
Maggie, Glasgow, MT

"Steve, I'll be honest: I came into your seminar saying, 'Why do I need this, I am NOT the problem…!' Imagine my surprise to find I AM the problem. Now I know, and now I have the tools to start fixing it. Thank you!"
Jenn, Bayonne, NJ

"Steve: Of all the gems I took out of your training, one of the best was "Stop wanting others to change – it will lower your stress level." You are too right! I've also found that if I make the effort to understand where they are coming from, the results can be very satisfying. I've seen you and Zig Ziegler a couple of times, and it's people like you who help us reinvent ourselves into the people we were meant to be. Thank you from the bottom of my heart!"
Bonnie, Portland, OR

"After having Steve Beck train our staff, our Customer Satisfaction scores skyrocketed!"
Sheila, Polson, MT

"Steve, I used to be a grouchy guy on a regular basis. After listening to you, I made it a goal to live my life to the fullest, not care what other people think of me, and provide everyone around me with the best customer service. My co-workers and clients realize I'm more fun to be around, and I'm not going to lie: my wife was a little freaked out due to my improved customer service! Thank you so much for changing my life."
Mark, Havre, MT

"Everyone from my company has taken or will take your seminars. You're my #1 resource in developing others to be great leaders! Thanks!"
Larry, Helena, MT

Copyright 2023 by Steve Beck

All rights reserved. No part of this book may be reproduced, transmitted in any form or by any means, electronic or mechanical, including photocopying, recording, or by any information storage and retrieval system, without express written permission from the author, including fair-use quotes when the source is also provided.

Published by Beck Seminars

Library of Congress info
Beck, Steve, 1953-
Life Is Short So Live It Now
101 Insights for Living Your Best Life
By Steve Beck

Printed in the USA
First Printing 2023

ISBN 978-0-9832008-5-7

Dedication

This book is dedicated to all those people who showed me HOW NOT TO BE and to all those people who showed me HOW TO BE. Thank you for showing me the way!

Steve Beck

Table of Contents

	PREFACE	13
1.	**PREPARATION**	15
	When Will YOUR Dreams Come True?	16
	The Seeds You Plant	17
	Like Water in the Desert	19
	Brand New Endings	20
	The Power of Positive Routine	21
	Being Lucky	22
	Affirm Your Day	24
2.	**FOCUS**	27
	FREE Personal Assistant	28
	Best Foot Forward	29
	Make Your Problem Your Opportunity	30
	Bring It Every Day	31
	In The Zone	32
	The Main Thing	33
3.	**POSITIVITY**	35
	Great Day Every Day	36
	Beautiful Choice	38
	"How Ya Doin'?"	39
	Fall In Love With Your Life	40
	The "Yes" Button	41
	7 to 1 Positivity	42
	Let Them Laugh	43
	The Blue Dot Theory	44

	Fall In Love With Yourself	47
	Shine Your Light	48
4.	**MOTIVATION**	**51**
	The One and Only Today	52
	Target Perfection, Achieve Excellence	53
	Worrying vs. Visualizing	54
	Downside to 100%?	55
	Let Defeat Inspire You	56
	Staying Focused	58
	Be, Do, and Have…Whatever It Takes	59
	When To Plant a Tree	60
	Be Inspired	62
	Your Habits and Your Life	63
	Script Your Play	64
5.	**LEADERSHIP**	**67**
	Shine and Share	68
	Level 1 and Level 2 Thinking	69
	Seven Tips to Leave Your Funk at the Door	70
	Individual Leadership	72
	Conquer Your Boulders: The Myth of Sisyphus	74
	One Person	75
	An Attractive Example	76
	Pride of Ownership	77
	The Courage Within You	78
	Constructive Criticism? It Works!	79
	Co-Worker Jerk Challenge	80

6.	**ACCEPTANCE**	**83**
	New Day, Same Old…?	84
	We All Want Four Things	85
	The Law of The Garbage Truck	86
	The AFL Principle	88
7.	**SELF-AWARENESS**	**91**
	Cause and Effect	92
	Attention Span Solution	94
	Intentional Living	95
	Two Wolves	96
	Start With Yourself	98
	The Gift of Listening	99
	The Dash	100
	'Have To' – or 'Get To'?	101
	Key to Happiness	102
	Insecure AND Fearless	104
	Enjoy Your Lessons	105
	12 Rules for Being Human	106
	Big Magic	107
	The Only Dance There Is	108
	We're All In This Together	109
	It's Your Perception	110
	No Mondays	111
	Be Aware	112
	Waking Up	113
	Do You Trust Yourself?	114

8.	**GRATITUDE**	**117**
	Honor Your Mother and Father?	118
	Our Own Groundhog Day	119
	Memorial Day	120
	Find Joy in All Things	122
	This Day: The Present	123
	The Perfect Age	124
	One Perfect Moment	125
	Smell The Flowers	126
	Blessed	128
	Backyard Inspiration	130
	Thank Your Parents	131
9.	**KINDNESS**	**133**
	Don't Be a Bug	134
	The Value of Caring	135
	Give a Smile	136
	They're Doing the Best They Can	138
	Everybody Has A Story	139
	That Little Bit of You	140
	Give	141
10.	**SELF-CARE**	**143**
	Vehicle of a Lifetime	144
	The Power of Meditation	146
	Be Your Own BF	148
	A Positive Breathing Exercise	149
	You're Always Right	150
	The News and You	152

11.	**CONNECTION**	**155**
	The All Approach	156
	Getting Together	157
	Great Customer	158
	What Goes Around	159
	Preserve Your Family History	160
	Wise Expectations	162
	Make A Difference	164
ACKNOWLEDGEMENTS		**167**

Preface

This book is a compilation of lessons and stories I have learned in my life. I thought at age 23 (when I met my teacher Ole Larsen) that I knew everything or almost everything. (I now know just how little I knew!)

These are insights I have been fortunate enough to gain over the past 40 years and it is my hope they resonate with you. I suspect there are plenty more lessons to be learned, so look for another book in the next few years!

I feel privileged to write this book and glad to finally get these thoughts out into the world.

It's a book you can pick up once in a while or grab a lesson once a day. Either way, I hope these insights provide you with inspiration for living your best life.

Enjoy and I hope our paths cross at some point in the near future.

With Love and Appreciation,

Steve Beck

1. PREPARATION

When Will YOUR Dreams Come True?

I'm a big fan of TUT: Notes From the Universe®. These statements are the creation of a guy named Mike Dooley (www.tut.com). I love this one about dreams so much, I have to share it with you. He said:

> *"Dreams come true, that's what they do. The only variable is when! For the slow approach for your dreams to come true: Resist. Insist. Deny. Stop. Second guess. Whine. Argue. Defend. Protest. Cry. Struggle. Ask others...when you already know the answer.*
>
> *For the quick approach for your dreams to come true: Visualize. Pretend. Prepare. Dodge. Roll. Focus. Show up even when nothing happens and give thanks in advance.*
>
> *You knew that.*
>
> *The Universe"*

Don't get caught in the quicksand of resisting and struggling to make things happen exactly the way you want them to in exactly the time that suits you. All you'll be doing is reacting to the negative influences and slowing down the fulfillment of your dreams.

Instead, focus on the positive, be prepared for anything at any time, and welcome it (what?) when it comes. Visualize all the best things you can dream of...you'll be amazed how quickly they'll come to fruition in your life.

The Seeds You Plant

Your mind is your garden, and YOU are the gardener. Of what? Of your thoughts.

What are you going to plant in your garden today? How about some positive thoughts?

A lot of people will say, "Well, if you don't plant anything, you don't get anything."

No, no, NO!

If you don't plant anything in your garden, you're going to end up with weeds, which are negative thoughts! Plant seeds of positivity in your garden.

Don't defend your negative thoughts - don't even let them come up. Don't give them any space in your garden. Have positive thoughts about yourself, your world, your family, your job, your co-workers, your friends. Plant positive thought seeds and cultivate those positive thoughts throughout the course of each day and you will have a beautiful garden.

Remember: garden, gardener. So, come on gardener, let's get to work – get those positive seeds in the garden!

Here are some "starter thoughts" for you, Gardener:

- Today is a Great Day, I am at my very best all day today.
- I am patient, positive, persistent, powerful, and disciplined.

- I am focused, effective, efficient, organized, and productive.

- I am in excellent health.

- Every day and in every way, I get better and better and better.

- I LOVE and APPRECIATE my life.

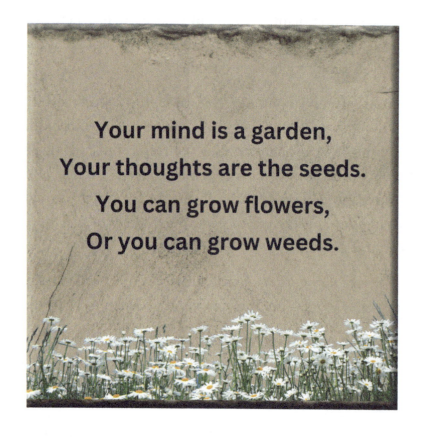

Like Water in the Desert

Did you know that the average person spends:

- Seven years in the bathroom
- Six years eating
- Four years cleaning house
- Five years waiting in line
- Two years trying to return phone calls to people who aren't there
- Three years preparing for meals
- One year searching for misplaced items, and...
- Six months sitting at red lights

WHAT?

Did you do the math? You realize, that's nearly 30 years?!

Like water in the desert, the time we have in our life is a finite resource. Treat that time and what you do with it like the precious resource it is. There is only so much of it available to us.

Poet Mary Oliver said, "What will you do with your one wild and precious life?"

Think about it…and make the most of it!

Brand New Endings

Here's a wonderful quote:

"Though no one can go back in time and make a brand-new start, ANYONE can start from right now and make a brand-new ending."

In short, you can worry about your past all you want… or you can focus on RIGHT NOW and what you do from this moment forward to make a great ending for yourself.

It's my plan to work on having a great day every day, between right now and the day I die. What a great challenge that is! Don't worry about your past. Don't let that influence right now…this moment…and your future. Be present. Be in the moment. Be here NOW.

That focus will support your efforts to have a great day today, tomorrow, this week, the entire year…on having a great life.

Didn't do it yesterday? That's OK – start NOW.

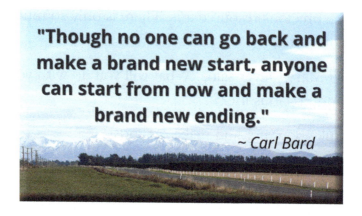

The Power of Positive Routine

Brushing your teeth…making your bed…taking a shower…eating breakfast. What do they have in common?

They're all routine things we do every single day and we would never think of not doing them! (Right?!)

How about thinking in a positive way today? You, getting your life on track by saying, "Today's going to be a GREAT day!" and you FIRING yourself up! Have that thought process become a routine like brushing your teeth, or taking a shower, or making your bed, which you do every day. (Right?)

Talk to yourself in a positive way (if you don't already) and watch how your life unfolds. It will become better and better and better, and more and more and more valuable. You will become the kind of human being that people will gravitate toward and want to be around.

"Try it: you'll like it!"

Being Lucky

Years ago, I heard that luck usually happens to someone who's very prepared. It's not about a four-leaf clover or a lucky rabbit's foot: you want to work on being very prepared. I'll tell you how to do it.

Over the weekend or whenever you have a block of days off, consider what you want to accomplish during the coming week. WRITE IT DOWN. Write down exactly what you intend to accomplish so that when your week starts, you hit the ground running.

This is something I do every single weekend and have for years. I spend an hour and don't allow any distractions: no emails, no phone calls, nothing. My entire focus is on what I'm going to accomplish in the coming week. It's basically setting myself up for accountability and it's great – it really helps keep me on track.

I highly recommend you do the same: prepare for the week on your days off. Spend a ½-hour or an hour – you'll find it's well worth your time. I predict you'll also be lucky!

"I believe luck is preparation meeting opportunity. If you hadn't been prepared when the opportunity came along, you wouldn't have been lucky."
Oprah Winfrey

"Luck tends to come to people who are prepared."
Gen. Colin Powell

Affirm Your Day

What is affirming your day?

It's simply you, writing out a list of positive statements each morning, and then reading that list out loud to yourself.

I'll share my list as an example. My list includes statements like:

Today is a GREAT day. I am at my very best all day and all night long.

I'm patient, positive, persistent, powerful, focused, disciplined, organized, generous and courageous.

I'm a wonderful father, brother, son, teacher, co-worker, friend, student, author, uncle, neighbor, and friend.

I am in excellent health.

This action is a VERY powerful tool! Your subconscious mind will listen to what it's being told, and it will follow those instructions. You can bring these things to fruition in your life and make it more wonderful than you could ever imagine.

Hey, Army Rangers do this. Navy SEALS do this.

How about you?

I recommend you do this every day for 28 days and you will start to see some of these things come to fruition in your life.

1) Today is a Great Day; I am at my very best all day and all night long.   TODAY'S DATE

2) I am patient, positive, persistent, powerful, organized, funny, effective, efficient, productive, disciplined, loving, caring, kind, supportive, understanding, considerate, strong, brave, honest, happy, generous & courageous.

3) I am in excellent health and weigh <u>IDEAL WEIGHT!</u>

4) I am an excellent Keynote Speaker, Seminar/Webinar Leader, Facilitator, Instructor, Consultant, Salesman & Trainer.

5) I am very successful; today I <u>SOMETHING FABULOUS</u>

6) Everyday and in every good way I get better, better & better.

7) My Net Worth is $ <u>YOUR IDEAL NET WORTH</u>

8) Something fabulous happens to me today.

9) I am a wonderful father, brother, son, husband, lover, friend, coworker, author, uncle, student, teacher, in-law, grandfather & neighbor.

10) I am great looking, sexy, slim & very attractive.

11) <u>Beck Seminars sales exceed</u> $ _____ in 202_

12) I Love My Life
    I Appreciate My Life
    I Love Steve Beck

Thank You God!
Thank You Florida
Thank You Steve Beck

Stephen H. Beck

An example of Steve's daily affirmations list. Use this as a starting point to create your own daily affirmations!

2. FOCUS

FREE Personal Assistant

Have you ever said to yourself, "I wish I was more organized"? Or "I wish I was more focused"?

I have a solution: hire a personal assistant!

You say, "Steve, I don't have enough time for that... enough money...are you kidding?"

No, no, no. It's FREE. That personal assistant lives within you, okay?

Think about it: who knows your schedule better than you? No-one!

You want to plan your week on the weekends and be really focused. Hit the ground running on Monday morning. You want to plan the next day, the day before - what you'll do that next day.

Work with your "personal assistant" to make sure you are super focused every day, so that on Friday afternoon, you look back on your week and you think, "Wow, I got a lot done! I WAS organized! I WAS focused. This is GREAT!"

It's a plan that works. Wake up (hire) a personal assistant – the one who lives within you.

You'll be surprised at what a difference it will make in your life!

Best Foot Forward

I want to share a piece of advice with you that I got more than 20 years ago. This came from my friend named Bruce Lay. At the time, he was one of the most successful real estate agents in Livingston, Montana. I'm pleased to report that he's still there, he's still doing it, he's still successful… and I have a pretty good idea why.

Bruce's advice? "Whenever you do something, put your best foot forward."

It's a simple statement – yet profound at the same time. To put your best foot forward is to lead with your best possible effort in anything you do. What a great goal and a great way to live life! I'll always remember the moment he said that.

Incorporate that thought into your daily routine. As you go about your day, remember to put your best foot forward. Do your best to be cheerful and then share that cheerfulness with others.

I've been working at it every day and will continue to do so. Thanks, Bruce!

Make Your Problem Your Opportunity

Did you ever consider that problems are perhaps opportunities in your life?

When you encounter a problem, you either run, complain, or reach deep inside yourself for the qualities you need in that moment: courage...tenacity...focus to solve that problem.

Since that's the case, then problems can be good things, right? They're opportunities for you to move yourself forward – opportunities for growth, because solving problems feels good.

I know we all sometimes say, "I don't want/need problems in my life"...but just think about how boring your life would be if you had no problems!

Problems require critical thinking to find solutions. They make you adapt. They force you to reach outside your comfort zone...and that's where the greatest growth in our lives can be found.

Face those problems. Get through those problems. Move on to bigger and better problems – and the growth they offer. That IS where the magic happens!

Bring It Every Day

You know, you've got to "Bring It" every day.

What does that mean?

To "Bring It" means to do your best every day. Every single day.

Think about all the championship-winning athletes you've heard talk. Do they say, "Well, we won the Super Bowl last year!" "Stanley Cup winners – woo hoo!"

NO. While they may appreciate the accomplishment, they're all about today's game….and what they have to do to "bring it."

Apply that attitude in your own life. Do you say, "I was 'Employee of the Month' last month!" That's fabulous – now, what about this customer walking in the door? What about that phone that's ringing?

You've got to bring it every day. You can't rest on your laurels. If you were fabulous in the past, that's TREMENDOUS. Now you've got a reputation to uphold!

So, what are you going to do today? What about this moment? What about this afternoon? Always remember to celebrate the victories and achievements…but don't rest on your laurels…don't allow yourself to get complacent.

Can we count on you? Will you continue to be excellent?

I know I'm going to work on it – I hope you will too!

In the Zone

What does it mean to be "in the zone?"

By definition, it's being "in a mental state that enables one to perform to the best of one's ability."

Have YOU ever been in the zone? That point at which everything seems to be working perfectly for you – everything's falling into place. When it happens, it's easy to get excited – and that's good. It's also easy to say, "Wow, what a coincidence – I can't believe that happened!"

The fact is that when that happens, it's not a coincidence. Instead, it's the realization of the efforts you've been putting forth to make each thing you do each day of your life great. Things are happening!

Don't worry about it, don't overthink it, and don't get in your own way. Let it flow.

Just look at the situation and say, "Yep. This is the way it's going to be from now on, and I like this!" The self-discipline you've displayed in your life is paying dividends. Keep up the self-discipline and enjoy being in the zone!

Remember: it's not a coincidence, it's your life working.

The Main Thing

"Keep the main thing the main thing."

Have you heard this expression? I heard it not long ago for the first time and I love it!

"Keep the main thing the main thing." What does it mean? Here are some examples:

If you've set a goal to lose weight in your life, don't lose your focus: keep the main thing the main thing.

If you've decided you want to make more money this year, don't let any setbacks derail your progress: keep the main thing the main thing.

If you've made a commitment to spend more time on your health and with your family -- you know things will come up to challenge your commitment, so remember: keep the main thing the main thing.

If you've made the effort to commit to what you want in your life, then you need to make sure to stay focused on whatever that is. Recognize that there will be challenges and you may have to make changes but keep your eye on that commitment.

Keep the main thing the main thing!

3. POSITIVITY

Great Day Every Day

Do you have a great day every day?

You don't? Why not? Think about it: is the alternative better?

Let's put it in perspective.

If you or someone you love is having heart surgery, you want the surgeon to be having a great day, right? (I know I do!)

If you're having a root canal, you want the dentist doing that work to be having a great day…

And what about the person on the assembly line who put your car together? You better believe you want them to be having a great day!

Whether you realize it or not, people want – they expect – you to have a great day; they really want you at your best, having a great day every day!

So, why wouldn't you have a great day every day? Remember, you're in charge of your own day and your own destiny – and we all know the alternative is NOT better!

Now: do you have a great day every day?

Of COURSE you do!

Beautiful Choice

We all have choices in life.

That's one of the most beautiful things in life - <u>you have choices</u>.

You have a choice over SO many things: to be happy – or to be sad. To be composed – or to be angry. To enjoy every day of the week equally – or to decide that Mondays are the worst. To love your body – or not. To be satisfied with your life – and not disgusted or frustrated with your life.

A choice. That's one of the most beautiful things we have as human beings.

I HIGHLY recommend that you choose the good stuff in life: how wonderful you are…how beautiful your body is…how grateful you are for all the positive things you have in your life.

Choose the good stuff. Remember: your choice is just that: <u>YOURS</u>.

"How Ya Doin'?"

I like to focus on the positive.

When people ask me, "How you doing?" sometimes I say "Well, you want to know how bad it is, or how good it is? Because it's just as good as it is bad and it's as bad as it is good. Which one you want?"

At that point, they usually say, "I just asked you how you're doing...!"

The truth is, when someone asks us "How you doing?" we could tell them how terrible our life is and focus on all our trials and tribulations. And after a while, they're reaction is "Oh my gosh, am I glad I'm not YOU!"...(worse yet, they even quit asking at all.)

So, when someone asks, why not focus on the positive, how wonderful your life is, and how lucky you feel in your life? Before long, their reaction will be "You lucky dog!" and "I want what they have!"

Hold the "poopy" stuff close to the vest and talk about the good things instead. Focus on the positive. Focus on the wonderful! We may have to look for the good things sometimes, but they're always there.

NOTE: If you are feeling terrible and depressed and a great friend asks, and you feel safe talking to them, then let them know what's happening so you don't keep it bottled up inside. Talking to good friends about your problems, frustrations and FUNK can really help.

Fall In Love With Your Life

Fall in love with your life.

What does that mean? Fall in love with your family. Fall in love with your friends. Fall in love with the people you work with. Fall in love with your customers. Fall in love with your house. Fall in love with your body. Fall in love with all those things around you. And then…

Fall in love with the person who checks you out at the grocery store. Or hardware store. Or the bank teller or at the credit union or at the casino. Fall in love with people that take actions to help you during the course of your day.

Of course, you don't want to say, "I love you!" (I don't necessarily recommend it. They'll probably think you're goofy.) But what you CAN do is look at those people. Really LOOK at them – make eye contact. Pay attention to them, show them respect, and say, "Thank you!" for what they've done for you. Think about it: what do you have to lose?

Put that into practice each day and before you know it, you'll be falling in love with everyone and everything. It's a good practice with countless benefits.

And while you're at it, make sure and fall in love with <u>yourself</u>. It's a GREAT place to start!

The "Yes" Button

Remember the "Easy" button that office supply company used in their commercials?

I recommend you imagine you've got a "Yes" button and pretend your "Yes" button is like the Universe answering any question you have!

It should be obvious that you want to make sure you don't ask your "Yes" button the wrong question, like, "Am I going to have a terrible day today?" "Well, yes!" See, that's a problem!

So, you want to make sure you pose the RIGHT questions to your Yes button! To get you started, here are some examples:

- "Am I going to have a great day today?"
- "Is my good attitude going to be contagious to the people around me?"
- "Is there something I can do today to make a positive difference for someone else in my life?"

You KNOW what the answers will be when you ask those positive questions: Yes, Yes, and YES!

Enjoy that "Yes" button and make the most of it every day!

7 to 1 Positivity

Did you know…

It's said that for every negative thought you have, you have to have seven (7) positive thoughts to balance it out?

Think about it: that's a pretty lopsided ratio! And I don't know about you, but if I've got to work that hard to balance out the negative thought, well…why not just focus on positive thoughts to begin with?

I highly recommend it! When you continually say positive things about yourself…when you look at your life and your thoughts…which ones feel better to you? (Umm…that should be a "no-brainer!")

Focus on achieving that balance. It won't take long before you find that your mind starts to come to the positive side all by itself.

Just imagine the positive power those positive thoughts will bring to your life!

Game on!

Let Them Laugh

Several years ago, I did a seminar at a bank in Bozeman, Montana. During one of the breaks, a woman came up to me — she was about 75 years old and so sweet — and she said, "You know, all the things you talk about, like being positive and making a difference in people's lives?" She said, "I do it. I do it!"

Then she put her head down and said, "But they laugh at me. They laugh at me!"

I said to her, "Well, I understand people laugh at you. We live in that kind of society — a critical and a wise-guy society. People think it's silly to put forth that effort."

Then I said to her, "You're not going to stop, are you? Because they laugh at me too for being positive! So, tell me you're not going to stop, right?!"

She looked back up at me and said, "Nope."

I gave her a big hug! I said, "Good! I'll keep being positive, you keep being positive, and together, we'll see what we can do to make a difference in the world." It was a wonderful exchange.

If you're positive, stay positive. People may make fun of you. So what?! Let them! As the saying goes, "You do you." Continue to stay positive. You're going to affect people in a positive way.

The Blue Dot Theory

Have you ever heard of the "Blue Dot Theory"? It goes like this.

There was a blue wall and I painted it white and I'm kind of excited about showing it to you. Are you ready?

Here you go! What do you think?!

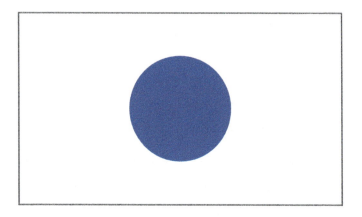

Let me ask you something: did your attention go to that blue dot? That's why it's called the Blue Dot Theory. We have a tendency to immediately notice what's wrong in our surroundings, in other people, and in ourselves.

For example: when you walk into somebody's home and you see a picture that's crooked, you mentally say, "Look at that picture!" You notice it when it's crooked.

If someone you were having lunch with had a piece of lettuce in their teeth, you'd be like "What?!" It would stick out to you.

When you're coming to a four-way stop and somebody blows the stop sign? You sure notice when someone does that…but when they don't and they DO stop like you expect they will? I'll bet you don't say, "Look at that, nobody blew the stop sign – everybody stopped!"

So, it's true and it's human nature: we have a tendency to notice what's wrong in people and in ourselves too. When you are in front of a mirror in the morning, what do you notice? Do you notice how beautiful you are? How great you are? How wonderful you are? Or do you notice all the blue dots: that you're getting older? You've got a double chin? You're losing your hair? You're getting chunkier?

Don't get distracted by the "blue dots" around you. Instead, look at how great your life is…how powerful and how thoughtful, how kind and considerate you are, and how wonderful life is…and then share that positive perception with others!

The Law of Attraction

You've heard of *The Law of Attraction*, right?

The Law of Attraction is a concept which says whatever you think about the most will be attracted to you.

If you think in a negative way, you'll have negative experiences and negative people in your life.

If you think in a positive way, you'll have positive people and positive experiences. (Of the two options, I'm guessing the positive is the one you want in your life!)

It's simple. Focus on thinking in a positive way today… tomorrow…this week…one day at a time and see what happens. See what – and who – you attract!

Fall In Love With Yourself

Have you ever considered falling in love with yourself?

There are so many things to love in life: cars, food, money, nature, people, pets, sports, clothes, your new phone…

What about YOU?

Fall in love with yourself. Fall in love with your amazing body. Fall in love with where you live. Fall in love with the fact you have a job and you're making money and you have healthcare…all these things that you have in your life! Begin to appreciate yourself and your life like you have never before done in the past.

Fall in love with yourself. How great you are, how wonderful you are, how thoughtful you are, how caring you are.

Fall in love with <u>yourself</u>.

Shine Your Light

Remember the book and movie *The Secret*® by Rhonda Byrne? The messages they contained were all anybody could talk about for a long time…and they are all still incredibly relevant. Every day.

Here's a favorite passage of mine from the book:

"You can change the path of your life from dark to light, or from negative to positive. Every single time you focus on the positive, you're bringing more light into your life. And you know that light removes all darkness. Gratitude, love, kind thoughts, words and actions bring light and eliminate the darkness.

Fill your life with the light of positivity." (*The Secret*, Day 25)

It's all about gratitude. Love, kind thoughts, positive words and actions all bring light to darkness. Let's focus on shining our light.

Every day!

4. MOTIVATION

The One and Only Today

Good morning!

Hey, you know what? We'll never have a chance to do this day over again. The possibilities and opportunities of this day are endless. You want to make sure you see them, grab them – and do something positive with them.

When today turns into tomorrow, it's going to be yesterday, you see? (Stay with me here!) So, we only have this day ONCE. There are NO "do-overs"! Make the choice to live today and give it your absolute best. Don't let those opportunities go by – grab them and do something positive any time you can.

Maybe the opportunity is simply to say "hello" to an older person. Give them a little "Hi, how are you today?" And then, really listen to what they say. Or…hold the door for someone. Pay a compliment to a co-worker. Or – be really friendly when you go home tonight! (How's that for ya?) "To my family, Steve?!" YES! Really friendly! When they say, "How was your day?" say "It was GREAT, how was your day?" And then, really listen.

Because…

We only have THIS day…

ONCE.

Target Perfection, Achieve Excellence

Bart Starr, future Hall of Fame quarterback for the Green Bay Packers is at his first meeting with the team's Coach, future Hall of Famer Vince Lombardi. Coach Lombardi says this:

"This team will work at perfection. Knowing we cannot achieve perfection, we will attain excellence."

It's a great goal for a team on the field - and a great way to live your life.

Work on perfection, on doing things perfectly. Knowing that perfection is not attainable, you will achieve excellence. And don't you want to have a life of excellence?

I'm guessing you do - I know I do.

Let's do this: let's achieve excellence!

P.S.: *Did you know…The Green Bay Packers, led by Coach Lombardi, went on to win 2 of the first 3 Superbowl's?*

Worrying vs. Visualizing

Do you worry?

Worrying is living in fear. You're focused on and picturing all the things you DON'T want to happen…and if you're like most of us, that probably generates anxiety.

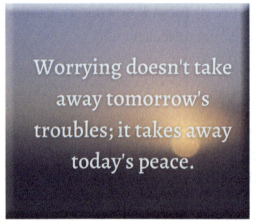

Visualizing is a positive way to distract yourself from that anxiety. Stop worrying. Don't live in fear. Instead, paint an image of positive actions and outcomes and imagine something you DO WANT to happen.

Focus on positive visualization. It's a great practice. It puts the power in your hands and the choice is YOURS. Should that fear come up inside of you, make it automatic. Flip that switch and go directly to how you'd like things to be. Visualize a peaceful place or a great outcome.

Visualize yourself having and being and doing the things you want to have and be and do. Do this within the first hour of your day. Visualize your day going GREAT and see what happens. It's all about taking charge of the day and creating the life you want and deserve.

Downside to 100%?

What's the downside to you giving your life 100%?

What I mean by that is giving your relationships 100% - being a fabulous spouse, partner, boyfriend, girlfriend.

Being a great co-worker: getting back to people right away, smiling when you walk in the door, having good energy.

Giving 100% when you're with your kids or your friends.

What's the downside of you giving your health 100%? IS there a downside?

Remember: our life is in front of us. This is the real thing – there is NO dress rehearsal. Make it a point to give your life 100%. Today, tomorrow, the next day. All week, all month. The next quarter, the next year!

Give it 100% and find out what the results are, because whatever you put out comes back to you tenfold, and sometimes one-hundredfold.

Watch how your life truly unfolds and develops when you give everything in your life 100%!

Let Defeat Inspire You

What's your "M.O." when you experience defeat in your life?

Do you curl up in a ball and hide from the world? Or do you step back, consider what you may have learned from the experience, and try again?

The following list details some of the failures experienced by a man who, by all accounts, was a HUGE failure. He is also an example for all of us:

- He failed in business in 1831.
- He was defeated for the legislature in 1832.
- He had a second business failure in 1833.
- He suffered a nervous breakdown in 1836.
- He was defeated for speaker in 1838.
- He was defeated for elector in 1840.
- He was defeated for Congress in 1843.

By now, wouldn't you think, "Stay down! Quit!"? But he forged on:

- He was defeated for Congress in 1848.
- He was defeated for a Senate seat in 1855.
- He was defeated for the Vice Presidency in 1856.
- He was defeated for another Senate seat in 1858.

Who was this HUGE failure? All of these things happened to Abraham Lincoln – before being elected President of the United States in 1860.

Don't let defeat get the best of you. Look for the lessons and let them inspire you to keep going! Believe that giving up is not the answer, that weaknesses can be turned into strengths, and that failing is better than not trying at all.

If Abraham Lincoln could do it…then so can we.

> "Do not judge me by my successes, judge me by how many times I fell down and got back up again."
> — Nelson Mandela

Staying Focused

I want you to think about staying focused and what that means.

So, you've set your goals for the year. You're fired up, you're ready to go, and what happens? You get derailed. You stop. You quit on yourself.

How do you get past that?

Pick yourself up and get back in the race. Make the effort to live a life of intention every day. Get focused, get fired up, and do NOT quit on yourself.

Do you feel that no one cares if you achieve your goals? They may not…but YOU do. You're the one who cares the most and that it matters the most to, because at the end of the year you want to be able to look back and say, "YES – I OWNED this!"

So, don't quit on yourself. Keep going.

That exercise program you promised yourself you'd do…the improvements you set out to make in your diet…going back to smoking after you promised yourself you'd quit. It happens to ALL of us.

If you're off track, do NOT beat yourself up over it – it's done. Don't get caught up looking backward and worrying about it!

Instead, get back to your intention, refocus, recommit yourself. (Remember, it's not about what's happened, but what YOU do about what's happened.)

You've got this!

Be, Do, and Have…Whatever It Takes

I believe there are moments in life where we all say to ourselves: "I want it, but I'm not willing to do what it takes to get there."

Think about it. We want to lose weight; we want to be in shape and be healthy…but do we want to go to the gym regularly? No. Do we want to impose restrictions on our diet and give up the goodies like peanut butter…chocolate…ice cream? No way!

"Work harder than you did yesterday if you want a different tomorrow."

Setting those goals for yourself is GREAT! But once you do that, you also have to be willing to do what it takes to get there. Change doesn't happen on its own and you must be willing to face frustration and failure to get to the other side and be, do, and have what you want to be, do, or have, to achieve your success and reach your goals.

Now is the time to get started – let's DO this!

When To Plant a Tree

Let's consider the idea of personal growth.

An arborist was asked, "When's the best time to plant a tree?"

His response? "20 years ago. But if you didn't plant it 20 years ago? Today."

You know, the same holds true for personal growth. So, you didn't work on "your life" 20 years ago…then start today!

It's a lot easier to do than you might think. Personal growth is about you working on you. Working on your future today. And if you work today, even a little bit – a little bit – it WILL make a difference. I guarantee it!

My morning routine consists of praying for 30 minutes, meditating for 20-30 minutes, and then affirming my day in writing. I write out 12 different affirmations, then read them as I underline them. And I even sign it – it's a contract I have with myself. I do that Monday through Friday and have for the past 15 years.

Affirming my day grounds me. It makes me feel centered. It's my way to grow: personally, professionally, mentally, spiritually.

But if you haven't done this in the past 20 years, or you used to and got off track…then start TODAY. It's never too late!

My results are:

I'm playing better golf than I have in my whole life because one of my affirmations is…*Every day and in every good way I get better and better and better.*

My doctor confirms I am in in great health. He said at my last physical, "You have the chart of a 30-year-old" because one of my daily affirmations is *I am in excellent health.*

I have a great day every day because another affirmation is, *Today is a Great Day; I am at my very best all day and all night tonight.*

Be Inspired

Just for today…be inspired. Be motivated. Don't wait for someone else to do it TO YOU.

If you can't fathom being inspired for a whole day, then start with one hour. Or five minutes! It doesn't matter, just set yourself the goal to be inspired, to be fired up!

Be excited about your relationships.

Be excited about your job.

Be excited about your life.

BE the one who's motivated and inspired and who motivates and inspires others, rather than waiting around for motivation and inspiration.

Try it. What do you have to lose?

Your Habits and Your Life

Our lives - your life and my life – are determined by our habits.

If you have good habits, you'll probably have a good life. If you have bad habits, your life might be disappointing. If you have great habits, you'll probably have a wonderful life…if you have sloppy habits…you get the idea!

So, take a look at your habits. Look at the things you do over and over each day. Take a hard look.

Which things are positive and serve you? Keep doing those things.

The habits that don't serve you? (Wait, they DON'T serve you?) You KNOW where this is going: STOP doing those things!

Sounds simple…may not be as easy as it sounds. We all know change can be difficult. But if you can manage to start by changing one habit – making one change in your life – chances are very good that it will make a HUGE difference in your life.

Think about it!

Script Your Play

I want you to think about your life as a play. You are, in fact, the Producer, Writer, Director, and Star of your play. Your play is called – well, start with your name, and then make it as creative as you want. (After all, it is YOUR story!)

Now, consider this question: what's in your script, in your play tonight? How about tomorrow? Tomorrow night? Next weekend?

I'll tell you what's in your script tonight: nothing! The next day? Nothing! Why? Because you haven't lived it yet!

How do you WANT it to be? You're NOT going to focus on the negative or depressing, are you? Think about it: how would you LIKE your script – your life to be?

If you want to have a fabulous life, then make it happen…remember, YOU'RE in charge of your life. This is YOUR play and you're the Writer, Director, Producer and STAR.

Make it a hit that runs indefinitely!

5. LEADERSHIP

Shine and Share

You know, when you're happy with your life, you go around and 'Shine Your Light'. You show you have enthusiasm and excitement for life. You turn people on! You are illuminating dark places inside of them. Suddenly, that dark space inside of them becomes illuminated! It's powerful stuff!

You've had this happen to you: you meet someone and you have a little interaction with them, even just for a few minutes. When they walk away, you say, "I don't know why, but I feel great when I'm around that person!" or "She makes me feel wonderful!"

You need to understand: YOU have that same ability to make people feel great. And I'm not talking about going to work tomorrow and saying "Hi, everybody, let's all hug!" You and I both know they're going to think you're nuts!

Instead, just make it a point to display enthusiasm and excitement with your life, and then share that with others. Have a great time at work! Have a great time with your friends! Have a great time with your family!

See what happens. Life will be a LOT brighter – for them and for you.

Level 1 and Level 2 Thinking

Are you familiar with the idea of Level 1 and Level 2 thinking? We all know people who think in each of those ways. Let me explain.

Level 1 thinkers talk about "I" and "me" a lot. They're self-absorbed; they don't see the big picture. The way they see things, there's them…and there's everybody else.

Level 2 thinkers DO see the big picture. They say "we" and "us" versus "I" and "me". Level 2 thinking shows in little ways and big ways: these thinkers push in their chair when they leave a restaurant. They hold the door for someone. They are great listeners, they are considerate and understanding of others. They understand we're all in this together and they realize that everything they do affects everyone around them in a negative or positive way!

How often do you actually THINK about your thinking?

Try it: think about your thinking this week. If you realize you are a Level 1 thinker ("ME!"), change your thinking and focus on Level 2 instead ("WE").

Elevate your thinking – it will elevate your life. Every day!

Seven Tips to
Leave Your Funk at the Door

"Leave your funk at the door." If you haven't heard me talk about it, that means drop whatever negative thoughts, attitudes, and baggage you are carrying around with you at the door each time you enter a new place.

Going in to work? Leave your funk at the door. (So, you're late because your kids missed the bus and you had to drive them to school and then got caught in traffic? Leave it at the door.)

Walking in the door at home at the end of the day? Leave your funk at the door. (Your spouse/partner/kids/dog can't help that you had angry customers or that your boss/co-workers are jerks. Leave it at the door.)

Visiting the hardware store/grocery store? Leave your funk at the door. (So, some moron cut you off and took the parking space you had your eye on? Not the clerk's fault! Leave your funk at the door.)

Here are seven ideas you can use to help make sure you can 'leave your funk at the door':

1. *Exercise. Move! Five days a week, do something to get yourself going.*
2. *Meditate. Daily. (OK, five days a week.)*
3. *Listen to classical music – or even SILENCE...and just relax.*
4. *Scream, on the way home, in your car! (Leaving the windows up or down is entirely up to you!)*
5. *Realize the people around you – your family, your friends, your co-workers, your customers - don't deserve your funk, okay? Spare them. They deserve the best you there is.*
6. *Deep breathe. Right now! Let's do it: in...and out. And... repeat!*
7. *Practice the AFL Principle. Accept, forgive, and love people... especially ones who are not like you. This applies to you too. Accept, forgive, and love yourself!*

Let's all leave our funk at the door. It's an opportunity to start with a clean slate – let's make the most of it!

Individual Leadership

Are you a leader? Do you demonstrate Individual Leadership?

I can hear you saying, "C'mon, Steve – I'm not a manager. I'm not a supervisor!"

You don't have to be either of those to demonstrate Individual Leadership. Individual Leadership is all about developing your own personal excellence and self-mastery. It's all about keeping yourself efficient, productive, motivated, and accountable. Sure, those traits will be useful if you're a manager or supervisor, but even if you're not: imagine the power they would bring to your life every day!

There are five areas to focus on to develop your Individual Leadership:

1. Be your absolute best throughout the course of the day – in everything you do.

2. Give exceptional "customer service" to every person you interact with throughout the course of the day, whether they're customers, co-workers, friends, neighbors, family members, even strangers.

3. Leave your FUNK at the door! At work and at home. Don't drag the "baggage" or bad stuff from the last place you were to the next place you're going: leave your FUNK at the door.

4. Take ownership of your life. Of the good AND the bad. Take ownership – after all, you're the one who makes your life great.

5. Be a shining example of what it's like to live with Elegance, Grace, Honor, Trust, and Respect.

Individual Leadership extracts your potential and polishes it.

Be an example of what it's like to live with Individual Leadership.

> LEADERSHIP IS NOT A POSITION OR A TITLE, IT IS ACTION AND EXAMPLE

Conquer Your Boulders: The Myth of Sisyphus

Are you familiar with the myth of Sisyphus and the rock?

Here is his story: The gods were displeased with Sisyphus, and as his punishment they dictated that he push a great rock up a hill. Even though the rock falls back down to the bottom of the hill each time, Sisyphus persists in his efforts – he gives the task everything he has.

We all have those rocks and boulders in our lives. The question is: what do we do with them? Do we choose to quit when the task seems too difficult? Or do we persist – like Sisyphus – and give it all we've got?

Let the story of Sisyphus inspire us. Do not give in to circumstantial disappointments – remember that they are only temporary. Let's accept our failures in the same way we accept our achievements. After all, they both provide learning opportunities.

And no matter how insurmountable the task may seem, we must never back down until we reach our potential.

One Person

Have you ever been at a job in which one person affects everyone else in a positive way?

One person can transform a whole department. One person can transform a whole location. One person can transform a whole team. One person can transform a whole company.

I've seen it done. I've done it myself.

That person could be you. Be pleasant. Be positive. Be upbeat. Be focused. Smile. (You know that a smile is the best gift you'll ever give or receive – and it doesn't cost a thing!)

If you're waiting for your co-workers or your boss or even the person leading your Zoom call to do it, don't. Don't wait!

If you come in with the attitude, "Let's do this, let's have a great day!" it rubs off on people. The nay-sayers will be upset, but the other 90% will appreciate it.

Be that one person. The one who transforms the whole department…the whole location…the whole team…the whole company.

Give it a try! Let me know what happens.

An Attractive Example

Every day, you're setting an example for others. We're all looking at each other and watching each other every day, and we're ALL setting an example for each other.

You want to set an example of elegance...grace...honor...trust. So, when people look at you, they think, "I like her", "That guy is great", and they almost want to BE you.

That's what being attractive is really all about: people are attracted to your personality. They want to be around you because it exudes out of you: that elegance...grace...honor...trust...respect. When you meet people like that, don't you find yourself drawn to them?

Don't take it lightly! I don't. I want to make sure I'm in a good mood and that I share that good mood with everybody I interact with throughout the course of the day. You can affect people in a negative or a positive way.

You want to make sure the effect you have is positive – that you're setting an attractive example. It's a matter of being part of the problem or part of the solution.

Your Choice!

Pride of Ownership

The term "pride of ownership" is often associated with real estate, but it can also apply in your profession or position where you work. No matter what your role within the company may be, make it a point to "act" as if you "own the place."

This means taking pride in your work, your colleagues, and those you serve...and doing so with a sense of gratitude. Put your best effort forth in every task you do, no matter how big or small. As you encounter fellow employees, say, "How are you?" When you see a customer, whether they're a first-timer or a repeat, say, "Thanks for coming in." There is a sense of joy that comes with taking ownership of something that's deemed valuable...and all those things are valuable, aren't they?

Treat everyone you encounter with respect and enthusiasm and show them you're excited that they're there. By extension, you're also showing that YOU are excited to be there. Do it today. Do it tomorrow. Do it this whole week – for the rest of the month – for the rest of the year.

It will get easier to do every day and it WILL change your point of view.

The Courage Within You

Always remember…

The same courage that was within Rosa Parks on December 1, 1955 - when she declined the order to give up her seat on the bus to accommodate a white patron - lies within you.

The same courage that Lou Gehrig displayed as he made his "luckiest man in the world" speech - after he'd been diagnosed with a debilitating disease that was killing him - lies within you.

That very same courage lies within you. You can call upon it at any time to help yourself. You can even share that courage to help those around you. It may appear in greater or smaller measure depending on the situation, but that courage lies within you. Never forget it.

Be courageous…especially when every instinct is telling you to run the other way and you don't think you can do it.

You can. That courage lies within you – today, tomorrow, always.

Constructive Criticism? It Works!

Constructive criticism. It's a unique and powerful concept when applied correctly!

When you are ready to complain about a situation, look for a logical solution too. So, rather than unloading on someone about a problem, make it a point to come up with a solution and present that along with your complaint.

It might sound strange, but you'd be surprised how effective the practice can be. When I first learned about the idea in my 20s, I thought, "That's a good idea!" Fact is, I was a champion complainer. I was REALLY good at complaining.

Somebody finally said to me, "You know, you complain a lot. Did you ever think about trying to come up with a solution *before* you complain?" That feedback definitely changed the way I think. When you consistently work both the problem AND the solution into the discussion, no matter how big or small, you'll soon be thought of as a positive, go-to person in a tough situation.

How's that for a positive outcome?

Co-Worker Jerk Challenge

A frequent question I hear in my seminars is, "How do I deal with a co-worker who's a jerk?" "How do I handle somebody who doesn't get their work done?"

I bet you can relate – we've all got them (or have had them):

That co-worker who talks incessantly, WAY too loud, and is disruptive to everyone else's workflow.

The one who spends more time making personal calls than they do fielding calls from customers.

The one whose grooming habits leave something to be desired – or they indulge in them at their desk during work hours.

The one who spends loads of time on their phone checking Facebook, TikTok, the cryptocurrency market or just texting their friends.

They don't carry their weight; they don't do their part. They get paid like the rest of us, but the rest of us are the ones doing THEIR work in addition to our own. It's nuts!

You know what? Sure, it feels like those people are put on Earth as a test, just to see if you can handle it…and here's how you handle it.

You focus…on your own job. You focus on the positive. You focus on doing the best job you can every day and don't let them derail your efforts. There's a saying about concentrating your efforts in "keeping your side of the street clean." Remember, you can't keep your side of the street and theirs clean at the same time, and it's not your job to do so.

You do you, and don't let them get in your way.

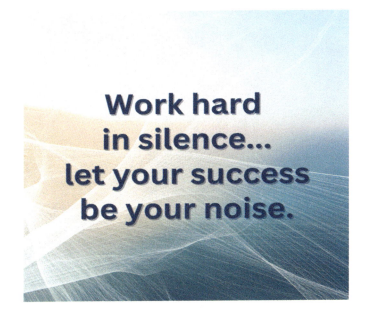

6. ACCEPTANCE

New Day, Same Old…?

There's an old saying: "the more things change, the more they stay the same."

Check out this passage:

> *"Our Earth is degenerate in these latter days. There are signs that the world is speedingly coming to an end. Bribery and corruption are common. Children no longer obey their parents. Every man wants to write a book, and the end of the world is evidently approaching."*

When do you think that was written?

Maybe by the Mayans, as they talked about the end of the world – projected for December 31, 2012?

Nope. That passage was written on an Assyrian clay tablet more than 5,000 years ago. Think about it! Even then, there was a school of thought that "things are going to hell in a handbasket" and the world was coming to an end.

Sound familiar? Seems like there are many who think that's exactly what is happening today and it's all too easy to get caught up in that line of thinking.

The next time you find yourself thinking that way, don't forget to breathe…everything is fine!

We All Want Four Things

We are all in this together.

There are Jewish people, there are Christians. There are people who are old, there are people who are young. There are people who are black, there are people who are white. There are people who are rich, there are people who are poor. There are Republicans, Democrats, smokers, non-smokers…

As the saying goes, "there are two sides to every coin"… but the truth is, we are all in this together.

So, forget the "blame game". Don't complain about the other person and point fingers. Instead, remember that everybody wants four things:

1. *To be loved*
2. *To be hugged*
3. *To be cared for*
4. *To be included*

EVERYBODY.

We're all in this together. Let's act that way. Like we're a family.

Let's learn to accept people who are not like you. Forgive them for not being more like you. It's OK that they're not like you! And once you do that, if you can learn to love them, so much the better – for you and your world!

It's a great challenge. Let's give it a shot!

The Law of The Garbage Truck

One day, a man took a taxi to the airport. During the ride, a car pulled into traffic right in front of the taxi. The taxi driver had to slam on his brakes – he skidded and missed the car by mere inches! The driver of the offending car then proceeded to start yelling at the taxi driver and his passenger!

Instead of getting upset, the taxi driver just smiled and waved at the other driver. He was really friendly! The passenger observed this and asked his driver, "Why are you being so pleasant to that guy? He almost ruined your car and could have sent us to the hospital!"

The taxi driver responded and shared "The Law of the Garbage Truck" with his passenger. He explained that many people are like garbage trucks. They run around full of frustration, full of anger, full of disappointment - full of garbage. Their garbage just piles up and they need a place to dump it…and sometimes they'll dump it on you.

If that happens (and it will), don't take it personally. It's not about you. Instead, just smile, wave, wish them well and move on. Don't take their garbage and spread it to other people at home, in the store, on the street. Successful people do NOT let garbage trucks take over their day. Life's too short, especially when you wake up in the morning with garbage-borne regrets, so love the people who treat you right and pray for the ones who don't.

Remember: Life is 10% <u>what</u> you make it, and 90% <u>how</u> you take it!

The AFL Principle

What is the "AFL" Principle?

AFL stands for "Accept...Forgive...Love." What does it mean to 'accept, forgive, love'?

First: accept people who are not like you. They are not the same color as you. They don't come from the same culture as you. They don't have the same religious beliefs as you. They're not the same gender, they don't have the same hairstyle, they don't dress like you, they don't have the same kind of family you do...you get the idea. Accept them and then forgive them.

Forgive them for what? Forgive them for not being more like you! You know you've done it – we ALL have! When you find yourself thinking, "They'd be a lot better off if they only [fill in the blank with YOUR expectation]", stop. STOP! That way of thinking is a trap! Don't let yourself fall into it. It does a disservice to you, to that person, and to your attitude. Don't go there.

Instead: love them. Accept them exactly as they are. Accept the details or circumstances exactly as they are. And then...love them. It's easier to do than you think, and it makes your life – and the world – a better place.

(Remember, accepting doesn't mean agreeing...it just means accepting!)

7. SELF-AWARENESS

Cause and Effect

Some people have the process of cause and effect reversed. Take a look at the chart.

It shows the big "I" which is us and then the outer world that reflects our appetite, our body, our thoughts, our emotions, the day of the week. We have it backwards.

Many times, we think, "When the outer world happens in a negative way, it causes me to (re)act in a certain way." But is it always a foregone conclusion?

NO. Think about it: who is in charge of your actions or reactions? You are.

Who is in charge of your emotions? You are.

Who is in charge of your desires? You are.

Who is in charge of your reaction to the day of the week? You are.

Who is in charge of your thoughts? Your body? YOU are.

When you realize you may not always control WHAT happens but you CAN control your reaction, that's the moment at which you truly take charge of your life.

So remember: YOU are in charge of your life. YOU are in charge of your reaction to the outside effects that take place…those things are NOT in charge of your life!

Those things don't cause you to be a certain way…unless, of course, you let them.

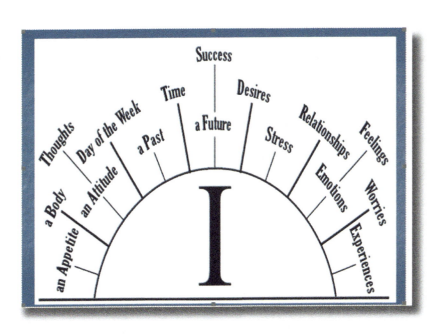

Attention Span Solution

Recent studies show that the attention span of the average person is 8.25 seconds. That's down from 12 seconds (in 2000)…and less than that of a goldfish: 9 seconds. That really isn't surprising, since everything around us has been reduced to "bite-sized" chunks or quick snippets or sound bites.

So, how do you develop better focus or get your focus back when you're losing it?

Practice being mindful. Be present, be in the moment. When you're listening to someone and you suddenly sense your attention floating away to think about how much you'd like a cup of coffee or an item you need to add to your shopping list or that you need to stop and fill your car up with gas…

Bring yourself back to the present moment. Whether it's to the person in front of you or a task you're working on, mentally circle back and say to yourself "This is the most important thing in my world at this moment in time."

You'll be amazed at what a difference developing that discipline as a routine can make in your life – and in your relationships with others! You'll be more focused and you'll be a better listener, and that's a gift.

Intentional Living

Have you heard of intentional selling? Intentional selling is when a salesperson gets on the phone and makes phone calls with an intention of what they want to accomplish – making sales -- versus just making the calls and crossing them off the list.

If you're a real estate agent, you show a house with the intention of selling it, not just showing the house to say you've shown the house.

What about Intentional Living?

Intentional Living is all about examining your 'why'. Ask yourself why it is you do certain things in your life, and make sure you're happy with the answers. (And be honest!) If you're living an Intentional Life, you're making it a point to make small, conscious daily decisions about what enhances your life versus what just clutters your life, distracts you, and pulls you off course from your core goals and beliefs.

Intentional living. You want to live this day, this week, this month, this year, with an intention. What would you like to have happen? How do you want to be? What do you want to become? It's a great way to live life…instead of just crossing another day off the calendar and saying, "Whatever!"

You want to define your priorities in life, get clear on what it is you want from life, and then live each day in alignment with those priorities. Intentional Living

Are YOU living an Intentional Life? If so, continue. If not, start today!

Two Wolves

The story of the two wolves is an ancient tale that has been a part of Native American tradition for generations. The exact origin of the story is unknown. I often share this in my speeches and seminars, and it is wisdom worth thinking about.

In a conversation between a grandfather and his grandson, the old man says, "I have a fight going on within me. It is taking place between two wolves. One is evil: he is filled with anger, envy, sorrow, regret, greed, arrogance, self-pity, guilt, resentments, inferiority, lies, false pride, superiority, and ego."

The grandfather looked at his grandson and continued. "The other is filled with positive emotions. He radiates joy, peace, love, hope, serenity, humility, kindness, benevolence, empathy, generosity, truth, compassion, and faith."

He added, "Both wolves are fighting to the death. The same fight is going on inside you, and inside every other person, too."

The grandson took a moment to consider these statements. At last, he looked up at his grandfather and asked, "Which wolf will win?"

The grandfather's reply was simple: "The one you feed the most."

It's easy to get beaten down by life and its circumstances, especially when they're not what you'd expected or hoped for. But it's important to remember that the events are not what has power over you – how you choose to react is what really matters.

Start With Yourself

In many of my training sessions, I share the message "Start With Yourself." These words are written on the tomb of an Anglican bishop, 1100 AD, in the crypts of Westminster Abbey:

"When I was young and free, and my imagination had no limits, I dreamed of changing the world. As I grew older and wiser, I discovered the world would not change, so I shortened my sights somewhat and decided to change only my country...but it too seemed immovable.

As I grew into my twilight years, in one last desperate attempt I settled for changing only my family - those close to me - but alas, they would have none of it.

And now, as I lie on my deathbed, I suddenly realize that if I had changed myself first, then by example I would have changed my family. From their inspiration and encouragement, I would have then been able to better my country and who knows...I may have even changed the world."

My advice? Don't worry about all the external things and the rest of the world.

Just worry about YOU, changing yourself, and then maybe...

You'll change the world.

The Gift of Listening

When we listen to someone, the idea is that we're creating a safe space for them to communicate into. If you're going to do that, you want to be a really good listener. Listening shows you care. Listening shows your respect. Listening shows that you respect and care about the person who's speaking to you.

If you're not a good listener and someone in your life wants to communicate a problem, what's going to happen? That person is going to walk away from you and they'll still have the problem. It could be that maybe you weren't the right person for them to talk to, which can happen, and that's OK. But perhaps they'll think that maybe <u>you</u> don't care about them. Is that what you want?

So, work on your listening skills. We have two ears and only one mouth for a reason: so we can listen twice as much as we speak! Be a great listener today. This week. This month. This year. Work on your listening skills. If you're a good listener, it shows you respect and care about the person who's sharing whatever they're sharing with you.

You never know when being a good listener will make a world of difference to someone!

The Dash

Have you ever considered the information shown on a tombstone?

Under the name of the person is their date of birth and their date of transition. Between their date of birth and their death is a dash.

That dash is really the most important part. Think about it: it's what separates the day we come into the world and the day we leave it and it symbolizes all the events that sum up our life! That dash represents our life on this planet. That dash represents the impact we've had on those around us during the course of our life.

How did we live our life? How did we choose to spend our time? That's all rolled up into that single dash.

It will be YOUR dash. Make it special, unique, and spectacular – make the most of that dash!

Keep in mind every moment of every day you have the chance to enhance that dash.

Let's do this!!!

'Have To' – or 'Get To'?

Here's a vocabulary check-up for you.

You want to replace the phrase 'have to' with 'get to' so it sounds like this:

- Rather than "I have to go to work tomorrow" replace it with "I get to go to work tomorrow."
- "I have to watch the kids" becomes "I get to watch the kids."
- "I have to go to the gym" turns into "I get to go to the gym."

Think about it. How would you rather approach life: thinking of all the things you 'have to' do? Or all the things you 'get to' do?

'Have to' sounds like an obligation…drudgery. Bor-ING!

But 'get to'? It's all about opportunity! Privilege! (And isn't that what each of those things mentioned above are?)

This is a little thought-trigger to keep in mind that allows you to reframe how you look at what you're doing in your life.

Give it a shot – see what happens!

Key To Happiness

In the very beginning, a long, long time ago, the Great Creator was creating everything. She had created the animals, the fish, and the birds — but no humans yet.

She held a huge meeting and asked the group, "I want to hide the key to happiness from the humans. What do you suggest?"

A brown squirrel piped up, "Give it to me, I'll bury it in the ground."

She said, "No, they'll probably find it there."

A blue whale said, "Give it to me, I'll bring it to the bottom of the ocean" and She said, "No, they'll probably find it there."

The proud and beautiful eagle said, "Give it to me, I'll fly to the moon", and She said, "No, they'll probably go there, they'll probably find it there."

Then this old groundhog, one with a big wooly, scruffy coat, walks up and says, "Bury it inside of them."

And the Great Creator thought about it for a little while and said, "Ahhhh...yes, I like that idea and so it IS."

The key to happiness is right underneath your nose. It's within YOU. Your job is to bring it out.

You want to be happy? Look INSIDE. Bring it out. Share your happiness with people.

It's so simple…don't you think?

Insecure AND Fearless

The late Penny Marshall of "Laverne and Shirley" fame was a producer, director, and actor. I cut this quote from her out of the newspaper:

"I am a strange combination of fearlessness and massive insecurity."

I can relate to that and bet you can too. Part of us is like a lion – fearless. Lord of the jungle! And part of us is like a mouse that's scared. That's the way it is – that's life! Even with massive fame and talent, Penny Marshall admitted it: massive insecurity!

You have to work through that insecurity. You have to go through that feeling of "you're not good enough", "you're not smart enough", whatever that limitation might be…so that you can get to fearlessness and achieve what you want to achieve. And only you know what that is.

But don't we all want to get past that little mouse to achieve what we want to achieve? Let's do that: believe in yourself and ROAR like a lion!

I've got it – you've got it – let's do this!

Enjoy Your Lessons

My friend Luis sent me this quote from a woman named Charlotte Joko Beck. (No relation!) She says:

"Life always gives us exactly what we need at every moment. This includes every mosquito, every misfortune, every red light, every traffic jam, every obnoxious supervisor or employee, every illness, every loss, every moment of joy…or depression. Every addiction, every piece of garbage, every breath!"

She also says, *"Every moment is the Guru."* The Guru, of course, is the teacher. So, the idea seems to be that in our lives, we're the students, and it's all one big lesson. The challenge comes in our ability to embrace that concept and the lessons that come our way.

Will you let the lessons disturb you?

Or will you embrace them for the learning opportunity they present and enjoy them?

The mosquito buzzing around you…the red light or traffic jam when you're in a hurry…the rude co-worker or salesperson you're faced with…they're all lessons.

What will YOU do with YOUR lessons?

12 Rules for Being Human

Ancient Sanskrit teaches the lesson of learning new experiences in life without any ego, which requires the ability to set aside any old, pre-conceived notions or ideas in order to become more accepting of the new. This concept is closely aligned with Eastern Religion and Buddhism.

Consider these 12 rules for being human, as handed down from ancient Sanskrit:

1. You will receive a body.
2. You will learn lessons.
3. There are no mistakes, only lessons.
4. A lesson will be repeated until it is learned.
5. Learning lessons does not end.
6. "There" is no better than "here".
7. Others are merely mirrors of you.
8. What you make of your life is up to you.
9. Life is exactly what you think it is.
10. Your answers lie inside you.
11. You will forget all of this.
12. You can remember it whenever you want.

Big Magic

Did you know...

You have treasures hidden inside of you, and those treasures hope you have the courage to bring them forth?

This is one of the ideas author Elizabeth Gilbert talks about in her book *Big Magic: Creative Living Beyond Fear* (2015).

Gilbert says:

"I happen to believe we are all walking repositories of buried treasure. I believe this is one of the oldest and most generous tricks the universe plays on us human beings, both for its own amusement and for ours: The universe buries strange jewels deep within us all, and then stands back to see if we can find them." ("Big Magic", p.8)

What an optimistic and wonderful way to look at life! My hope for you is that you go on the quest to open up some of those treasures – open up those gifts inside you that are just waiting for you to arrive.

You know, they're ready for you. Every day is your time to shine and show you're ready for them!

(Here is a little secret: one key to getting to where your gifts are located is to meditate.)

The Only Dance There Is

When I was in my 20s, I read a book called *The Only Dance There Is*, written by Ram Dass, a spiritual teacher. In this book, he wrote, "The only dance there is in this life is to work on yourself. You, working on you."

He said, "Don't worry about your parents. Did you ever try to change your parents?" That hit home for me, and I thought, "Yeah...that didn't work!"

Along the same lines, did you ever try to change your spouse? Doesn't work either, does it? How about your kids? Your friends?

The message is that the only person you want to work on in this life is you! You work on you. You're sculpting your life. At the end of your life, the goal is to have created a magnificent masterpiece. And how is that accomplished?

It's accomplished by you, sculpting your life each and every day. Make your life great, day by day.

So today, work on yourself and your life. And tomorrow. And the next day...and the next day. Next week. Next month. For the rest of the year...and the one after that, and the one after that.

Make every effort to work through your fears and roadblocks and focus on your sculpture – your life. I know it won't always be easy, but so what, this is your life we're talking about. Great accomplishments are never easy.

You with me?

We're All In This Together

Dr. Martin Luther King Jr. said, "If you don't make it, I don't make it."

Mother Teresa said, "I can do things you cannot, you can do things I cannot; together, we can do great things."

Albert Einstein said, "We have to do the best we can, it's our sacred human responsibility."

Do you see the common thread between each of these statements? All three were made by people who were "big picture" thinkers: they visualized – and understood - that we all play a part in our collective success.

None of us were here 100 years ago, and it's highly unlikely we'll be here 100 years from now. However, we are here NOW, today, and I believe we have a responsibility to each other to be great every day and to do our best every day. After all, those efforts don't just affect us, they affect everybody we encounter throughout the course of the day – throughout the course of our lives.

Be great. Be your best every day. Today and every day. Do it for the rest of your life...because we're all in this together.

It's Your Perception

Remember, life is NOT about what happened to you, it's your perception about what has happened.

Many people have had terrible misfortunes in their lives and are distraught by what happened to them in the past... and some people let it go, like water off a duck's back.

So, it's not what happened to you in the past, it's your perception of what happened to you in the past. You can always change your perception.

If you want to change how you think about what happened in the past, make it your mission to tell yourself, "Well, that's the way it was." It's true. It's what happened, and there's nothing you can do to change it. (It's a lot like thinking you can go back and change something you read about in a history book in school!)

Accept, forgive, and love is the premise of what I call The AFL Principle:

Accept your past

Forgive the people that did you wrong – or even yourself – and then...

Love them – and love yourself – and move on.

Don't allow your past to determine your future; your future is bright. Don't give your past the opportunity to get in the way of that brightness.

No Mondays

Did you know: there's no such thing as Mondays?

Yes, you read that right! There's no such thing as Monday…or Tuesday or Wednesday or Thursday…or months of the year, or TIME.

I can hear you: "Steve, how can you say that?!"

The fact is, they're all labels, all invented, all created by human beings!

The idea that we all have an attitude about Monday is something WE'VE created: "Ugh, Monday!" But it's the same as a Friday, a Saturday, a Thursday.

We need to wake up to the fact that we're the ones who have a problem with Mondays…but there really is no such thing as Mondays! They're really nothing more than labels to mark the passage of time.

And wouldn't you rather live in the moment than worry about marking the passage of time? If you must have a day of the week, you can call it any day you want – as long as you have a GREAT DAY.

Be Aware

You want to be aware of <u>how</u> you do <u>what</u> you do in life: how you stand, your body language, how you speak to others, and perhaps most important, how you think. One suggestion is to live your life like you've got a Go-Pro camera over your shoulder recording everything you say and do. Do your thoughts and actions serve you and the life you're living?

Do you have positive thoughts about your life? Your family? Your job? If not, why not? There's a good chance the reason why not is YOU. Watch your thoughts! Remember, your word is law in your universe.

This can take a little time. Change your routine and change your thoughts. Put the effort into focusing on the positive rather than the negative. Doing so will pay off for you and everyone with whom you come in contact.

Waking Up

I want you to wake up. No, not the way you do when you get out of bed in the morning. (Although that's important too!)

I can hear you: "OK, Steve: what is it I'm supposed to wake up to?"

Wake up to what you want in your life.

I KNOW what you want. You want three things:

1. *You want to be happy,*
2. *You want to be satisfied, and*
3. *You want to know your life makes a difference.*

I am here to tell you: your life makes a HUGE difference – in a negative or a positive way! The question is, which way will it be?!

Wake up to the fact that your life makes a difference on everyone you encounter – even YOU. Wake up to the fact that every day is a new opportunity to have a positive impact on everybody you encounter.

Are you awake?

Do You Trust Yourself?

I've heard a lot of people say they don't trust others. (In many cases, I don't blame them.)

But maybe a greater question is: do you trust yourself? Do you trust that you will succeed? Do you trust that you will make the money you want to make? Do you trust that you'll be successful?

You know that nobody can do any of those things for you. Making money. Losing weight. Feeling happy or satisfied. You are really the only person who can do those things for you and guess what? All those abilities already exist inside of you.

It's up to you to dig inside yourself and pull them out. Would you trust somebody else to do that? Would somebody else even be able to do that? A personal or business coach possibly, but in the end it will be YOU who will do it!

Don't let doubt take control: trust yourself. You are successful, you are fabulous, you are wonderful! Trust yourself that you ARE all those things and that you will become the person you want to be, have the things you truly want to have, and do the things you truly want to do.

Trust yourself!

8. GRATITUDE

Honor Your Mother and Father?

In my seminars, I often share with people the habits and practices I use to start each day: Pray, meditate, affirm my day, stretch. Every day.

And people often ask me, "Why do you meditate? Why do you affirm your day? Why do you pray?" "How can you do all those things every morning?"

Doing all those things grounds me. They help me start out my day on a calm and positive note and share positive emotions with people throughout the day. But another big reason I work on having a great day every day is to honor my parents.

When I was very young (maybe 6 or 7) I heard someone say, "Honor your Mother and Father." I knew my parents, but I did not know what honor meant. Later on in life, I finally understood.

That understanding really had an impact on me, as I realized how important it was for me to act in such a way that would make them proud – that would honor them.

So, for me, working on having a great day every day is a way of honoring my mother and father, and saying "thank you" for the gift of life they gave me. Having a great day every day is a way for me to acknowledge and honor their gift. Since they brought me into this world, I will do my best to make every day count and to have every day be a Great Day. That is my gift back to them.

Our Own Groundhog Day

You know, we're all in the middle of our own personal 'Groundhog Day'. You remember the movie by that name starring Bill Murray? He lived the same day over and over and over…and over again.

You and I are in the middle of the same experience. Check it out:

- *Do you have the same house you did yesterday?*
- *Do you have the same car you did yesterday?*
- *Do you have the same job you did yesterday?*
- *Do you have the same body you did yesterday?*
- *The same partner or spouse or kids as yesterday?*

See, most of the time, it's true! Sure, the names of the days of the week may change, but the rest of it? Groundhog Day.

What do you do to break that loop – to change that cycle?

Appreciate your life! Appreciate the things you have and the people who are in it and then share that appreciation with others.

All it takes is that one moment of appreciation to propel yourself forward in your fabulous life!

Memorial Day

Did you know...

Memorial Day was originally called Decoration Day? That name came about based on the tradition of decorating the graves of those who died in war with flowers, wreaths, and flags.

Memorial Day is the day on which we remember those who've given their life for our country...for our freedom. My brother was one of those: he was killed in Vietnam five days before his 21st birthday.

Memorial Day is so much more than the 3-day weekend we've all come to treasure and enjoy. On the next Memorial Day, look for events in your community and take part in a local parade, or a ceremony of remembrance in your town. Fly a flag.

Send out this thought: to all the soldiers who gave their lives for our freedom, we say thank you. We remember you. (We might not say it enough, but I'm confident we all think it.)

And to all the men and women who are serving right now in the military...to make sure we are safe, we are free... thank you.

Thank you so much for your service. We appreciate you.

Vietnam Veterans Memorial

*Rubbing of Steve's brother's name from the
Vietnam Veterans Memorial in Washington, D.C.*

Find Joy in All Things

I was talking with a friend on the phone recently and she said something that struck me as so profound that I wrote it down and have it hanging on the wall in my office.

She said, "Find joy in all things."

"Find joy in all things?" I replied. "But…I get really angry sometimes! Find joy in all things? In the good things, sure, but in the bad?"

Find joy in all things.

Apparently, the Universe was sending me a message because right after that, someone sent me a Bible quote from James 1:2-3:

> *"My brothers and sisters, whenever you face trials of any kind, consider it nothing but joy because you know the testing of your faith produces endurance."*

The testing of your faith in anything develops endurance…it also develops character.

Find joy in all things.

Thanks, Universe – I'm listening.

This Day: The Present

"Yesterday is history, tomorrow is a mystery,
but today is a gift;
that's why they call it 'the present'."

Here it is! This day! It's here! It's finally arrived! It's what we've been waiting for our whole lives - this day!

I've heard the quote at the top of this page and have also heard people say, "This day is called the present and it's a gift from the Universe."

And "What you do with this day is your gift back to the Universe, so spend this day well."

Maybe…just maybe, our job here on Earth is to enjoy this day. Appreciate this day for exactly what it is.

So, this day -- this week – ENJOY. It's here, it's arrived, and it's called the present…for a reason.

The Perfect Age

Are you worried about getting older?

Don't be. Remember what Mark Twain said: "Growing old is a privilege denied to many."

Just like so many things in life, our age and how we feel about it all comes down to our mindset.

Turning 47 was a weird year for me, but I looked in the mirror that day and said, "47 is the perfect age – and I'm 47!" (Full disclosure: I did have to sneak up on myself to do that.) But I kept it up for that entire year.

When I turned 48, I remembered how the idea of the 'perfect age' felt, and said, "48 is the perfect age, and I'm 48. What a great coincidence!"

When my daughter turned 25, she said, "25? Oh, I'm sooo old!" (At 25!) Remember, it's all about our mindset.

Think about it: maybe the age you are right now is the perfect age…and on your next birthday, you'll be turning the perfect age…and so on. You get the idea: be present and embrace the moment, because whatever age you are, it's the perfect age.

One Perfect Moment

The front desk clerk at The Pollard Hotel in Red Lodge, Montana gave me a quote about having a great day.

She said, "One perfect moment in any day can make it a perfect day."

Think about it. All it takes is one moment. That one moment! We all get caught up in thinking the whole day has to be great, it's got to be perfect, and every single thing has to go our way. But what about that one moment?

She woke me up to realize that it's one perfect moment in the course of the day that we need to be aware of. That moment, when you look back on your day as you're about to put your head down on your pillow at the end of the night, focus on that one moment and say, "Yes, it was a great day."

Focus on how wonderful your life is. Focus on those perfect moments – because there are plenty of them on our journey...it's our choice what we do with them.

Smell the Flowers

Picture this.

16-year-old Steve is playing golf with his father, brother, and sister on a fabulous course at a prestigious local country club on a beautiful sunny day…and he's having a terrible game. Slices and hooks are plentiful…so is the swearing.

At one point, my father stepped in and said, "Hey, take it easy! Look around you. Look around!"

At that moment, he made me stop. I looked around and saw majestic oak trees, maple trees, weeping willows, colorful flowers, a beautifully manicured golf course. And my father said, "It's not always about the score. Sometimes you have to realize how beautiful it is on the golf course."

Sometimes the simplest wisdom is the most powerful. It was a metaphor for life and I realized that as I got older. When things get difficult, I need to take a moment to stop and look around… "Smell the flowers" as they say.

Let's all make it a point to appreciate all the beauty around us…let's smell the flowers. Let's stop our lives for a second, take a deep breath, look around and realize just how GREAT we have it. Let that feeling – and that understanding in -- and then share that with others.

That's our job…our responsibility.

Blessed

It never hurts any of us to be reminded to be appreciative of what we have. I share the following text, entitled *Blessed*, in my seminars. I've seen it attributed to a number of different sources, but the message is consistent. It says:

> *"If you woke up this morning with more health than illness, you're more blessed than the million people that will not survive the week.*
>
> *If you've never experienced the danger of battle, the loneliness of imprisonment, the agony of torture, or the pains of starvation, you are ahead of 500 million people around the world.*
>
> *If you attend a church meeting without fear of harassment, arrest or death, you're more blessed than almost 3 billion people in the world.*
>
> *If you have food in the refrigerator, clothes on your back, a roof over your head, and a place to sleep, you are richer than seventy-five percent of this world.*
>
> *If you have money in the bank and your wallet, and spare change in a dish someplace, you are among the top eight percent of the world's wealthy.*
>
> *If you hold up your head with a smile on your face and are truly thankful, you are blessed, because the majority can…but most do not.*
>
> *If you can read this message, you're more blessed than over three billion people that cannot read anything at all."*

Let in the appreciation of your life. Let it in and when it becomes overwhelming, let it out to whoever's in front of you. Share it! Face-to-face, over the phone, with your customers, co-workers, friends, family…even yourself. That appreciation is a gift – a blessing. Never hesitate to share it.

Backyard Inspiration

People often look to the famous (or infamous!) for inspiration. In reality, you usually don't need to look any further than your own backyard to be inspired. Inspiration is all around us! I know I've found it in my own friends, guys I went to grammar school with and have known my entire life. Here's just a few examples:

- Rick ran an Ironman Race…at age 60!
- Joe raised four foster kids…not one or two, but four!
- Toby regularly plays hockey…at age 67!

Looking for inspiration? Open your eyes and look – really look – at those around you. Your friends, your family, your neighbors, your co-workers. They're out there and they're doing great and amazing things.

Grab onto their positive example and be inspired to do your best every single day. And remember to not only thank them for their inspiration, but to share that inspiration with someone else who might be looking for it!

Thank Your Parents

At 27, I wrote my parents a letter to thank them for all the great things they gave me: the food, the bed, the education, the warmth...all those things and much more. I took the time to focus on those things and put them in a letter. And even though I thought I was doing it for them, I think I was the one who got the most out of it.

I highly recommend the exercise. And don't stress or be too sad if your parents are both gone. Take the time to bring them into your mind and imagine them sitting in a chair and you sitting in a chair facing them. And then thank them. They'll appreciate it and it will help you.

> During the 12 years I was involved in personal growth seminars, I remember my teacher saying to people who were angry at their parents, "Your parents did the best they could given the information they had at the time." That simple statement helped many people change their mindset.
> ~ SJB ~

If they're still around, then make the time to bring them to your house. Make them their favorite meal and tell them how much you appreciate all they've done for you.

If your parents live in a different state? Call them. Write them a letter. Surprise them with a visit! You'll be amazed at how much their gratitude will mean to you.

Your own attitude of gratitude can be invaluable when it comes to living your life to the fullest. Make it a point to share that gratitude with your parents or anyone who has contributed to your life!

9. KINDNESS

Don't Be a Bug

Karma.

You've heard of Karma. Karma says if you live a great life this life, if you're respectful and you're kind and thoughtful and generous with others, you'll come back and have an even better life.

If you don't live a great life and are disrespectful and always think about yourself first and you're not generous and are kind of a jerk to people…that's bad Karma. With bad Karma, you might not even come back as a human… you might come back as a bug.

Life can be tough enough as it is…you DON'T want to come back as a bug!

Karma is all about the actions we take, whether physical, verbal or mental. So, focus on good Karma: be kind and thoughtful and be sweet to people as you move through this life so you come back and have an even better life. (Don't be a bug!)

The Value of Caring

Let's consider the word "caring". Caring: "c-a-r-i-n-g". It's a simple word. According to Merriam-Webster, "caring" can be defined as: "feeling or showing concern for or kindness to others."

Caring is also powerful. Think about it:

If you want to give great Customer Service, you want to care about the customer.

If you want to have a great team, you want to care about your co-workers.

If you want to be in great health, you want to care about your body.

If you want to have a great family, you want to care about your family.

If any (or ALL) of those things are important in your life, then caring is so, so, SO important! It's an emotion that comes from your center, the very core of your being.

You want to care. Care for your friends. Care for the planet.

Let's all feel or show concern for or kindness to others.

Are you with me?

Give a Smile

A few years ago, I did some seminars for the staff at a casino. One of the attendees was a young woman whose job was to stand at the entrance and greet patrons as they entered. I knew she was greeting people as they came in and observed she didn't smile very much.

So, I said to her, "Hey, I'll be back to finish our training in one week. What I'd like you to do in this next week is smile at every single person who walks into the casino. As you say, "Hi!", or "Good morning" or "Good afternoon, welcome!" make it a point to look each person in the eye and smile, OK?" She promised she would.

When I came back for the follow-up training, the first thing this young woman said to me was, "Hey, Steve! Guess what?" (I already had a pretty good idea what she was going to tell me.) She said, "When I smile at people, they all smile back at me!" She was amazed and enthusiastic about the results she got. I thought to myself "What do you know?" and said to her "Congratulations – great job!"

This simple exercise demonstrated a simple truth in the world: when you smile at people, most will smile back at you.

When you are kind to people, most will be kind to you.

If you're considerate of people's feelings, most will be considerate of yours.

You've got to put it out there.

When you do, you'll find that it comes back to you tenfold…sometimes even one hundred-fold or more.

Do it. For them…and for yourself.

Be the reason someone smiles.

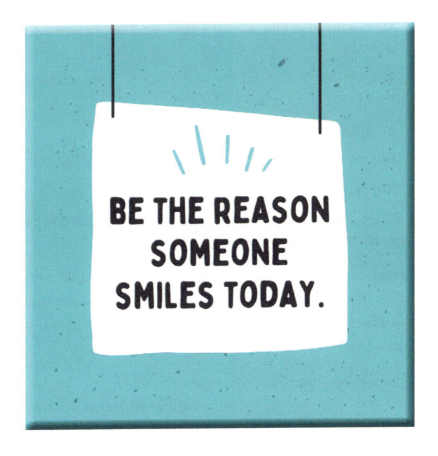

They're Doing the Best They Can

Here's a notion you might find hard to believe: the people you interact with throughout the course of an average day? They're doing the best that they can.

I can hear you now: "C'mon, Steve. Give me a break! How can that be?"

You say, "Wait a minute – my co-workers? They're doing the best job they can?"

"My kids? Doing the best job they can?"

"My neighbors? Don't even – please!? They're doing the best job they can?"

"The people that work for me? They're doing the best job they can?"

"My brother is…He's doing the best he can?"

"But my sister…! She's doing the best she can?"

"My parents?! They're doing the best job they can?"

When you're driving? "He – she – that jerk…?! They're doing the best job they can?"

Everyone is doing the best job they can. In that situation at that moment in time with the tools they have available. And when you look at life like that, your stress level will go waaaaaay down.

Remember how relieved you were when you stopped expecting other people to change and conform to your way of thinking and doing things? Life makes a lot more sense and is a lot less stressful when you give 'em a break, cut 'em some slack, and remember: we're all doing the best we can!

Everybody Has A Story

One fact of life we all need to realize is that we're all in this together. The people you live with, the people you work with, even strangers – they're going through a lot of different things, and often the same things you're going through!

We've all got issues…we've all got problems. Everyone's got a story. Some of them are sad, some of them are difficult, and some are just horrendous. And we all have that. You just never know what someone is dealing with.

Make the effort to be considerate of other people's feelings and treat people with kindness, knowing that they have a story behind that beautiful face of theirs. Sometimes people mask their struggles well. When you ask, "How are you doing?" they invariably respond "Good!" and that they're the happiest person in the world…but the fact is, everyone's got a story.

Make it a point to be just as kind, thoughtful, and considerate as you can to every person you meet every day. It's true: you may not get it back. But then again, it may come back to you when you least expect it – and need it most.

That Little Bit of You

I was presenting a seminar in Connecticut and when I asked for questions and feedback, one of the attendees raised her hand.

She said, "Everything you're talking about, my grandmother shared with me when I was growing up." I asked her to elaborate further.

She said, "My grandmother said whenever you meet somebody, you leave a little bit of yourself with them, and they leave a little bit of themselves with you." She got emotional as she shared the rest of her grandmother's advice: "Whatever you leave someone with, that little bit of yourself you leave with them, make sure it's your best."

She was right - what a great lesson. (Thank you, grandmother!)

And it's true: when we meet somebody, we leave a little bit of ourselves with them. What we always want to do is make sure the little bit of ourselves we leave the other person with is our absolute best.

Don't you agree?

Give

Never be afraid to give and don't resist the impulse to give.

Try it. Pick a worthy charity and give them $25 today. Or if you're walking down the street and see somebody begging, give them loose change out of your pocket or even a few bucks.

When I suggest this to people, they usually say to me, "You know what they do: they just spend it on drugs or alcohol." I actually DON'T know that. Sure, they may spend it on drugs or booze…but maybe my money goes to their family. Or maybe my money goes to them getting a pair of warm gloves or a hat or finding a good meal.

If you're not comfortable giving to someone on the street, then look for a charity that supports a cause you believe in and donate there. Today. Either way, you can be confident that you're giving to someone who needs it more than you do at that moment in time…and that can be a pretty great feeling.

10. SELF-CARE

Vehicle of a Lifetime

Remember what you felt like when you got your very first car? I'm guessing you loved it, you babied it, you treasured it, you gave it all the care it needed. You wanted to take good care of that vehicle so it would get you where you wanted to go.

Treat your body the same way. This week, this month, this year, take care of your body. After all, it gets you where you want to go, right? Treat it like the treasured vehicle it is!

If you don't already do these things, I highly recommend you incorporate them into your routine:

- *Take Vitamin C, D, and Zinc to boost your immune system.*
- *Eat the right foods to fuel your body – your vehicle – effectively.*
- *Ease up on your sugar intake.*
- *Get plenty of rest.*
- *Get a massage on a quarterly basis.*
- *Tell yourself daily that you are VERY HEALTHY!*

My father once said, "You can be a multi-millionaire, but if you don't have your health, you have nothing." As I get older, I understand just how right he was.

Take care of this vehicle of yours – this body – to make sure that you're in the best health possible and that you stay that way. It's an important vehicle.

Don't you think?

The Power of Meditation

Meditation. Transcendental Meditation. To transcend, by definition, means to go beyond human limitations and to break boundaries.

There are many well-known people who practice Transcendental Meditation (or TM): Jerry Seinfeld does and has for the last 40 years. Oprah Winfrey. Katy Perry. Even the Beatles did TM! It's a practice I <u>highly</u> recommend.

Transcendental Meditation is 20 minutes in the morning, 20 minutes in the afternoon. Thank goodness for Google: if you don't now meditate, Google "Transcendental Meditation" and read about it. Do a class on Transcendental Meditation. Make this year the year you begin to meditate. Make it the most important thing in your life (really?) to meditate every day. You'll see a positive change in your life that you can't even imagine.

Meditation is VERY powerful. You're accessing the power that exists inside of you when you meditate. You become much more in control of your thoughts when you meditate. For me, I'm a better father…husband…I'm more present in the moment…I'm more focused…all as a result of meditating. It's a practice that has changed my life. I've been doing it for more than 15 years.

Still not sure? Then ask yourself this question: Do you have the desire for stress release, inner peace, and stability in yourself? How about reducing stress to reduce anxiety as well as increasing focus?

If you already meditate, you know what I mean: I bet it's the most peaceful part of your day (it is for me!)

Meditation. "Try it, you'll like it."

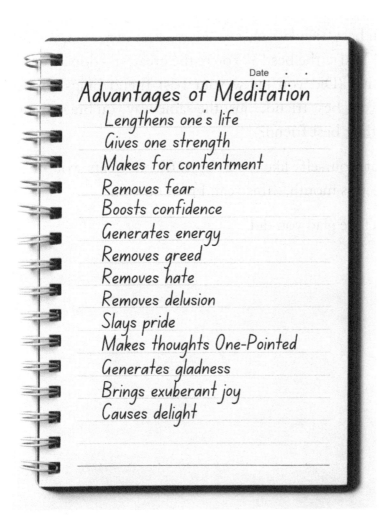

Advantages of Meditation
- Lengthens one's life
- Gives one strength
- Makes for contentment
- Removes fear
- Boosts confidence
- Generates energy
- Removes greed
- Removes hate
- Removes delusion
- Slays pride
- Makes thoughts One-Pointed
- Generates gladness
- Brings exuberant joy
- Causes delight

Be Your Own BF

I want you to treat yourself like your best friend treats you.

So, when you make a mistake or something, and say, "I'm so stupid!" "I'm such an idiot!" "I should have known about that deadline!" stop and ask yourself: What would my best friend say to me right now?

Your best friend would say "Hey, take it easy, man, you're fine!" "You're the best!" "You're the greatest – don't worry about it!" (Did you know your best friend brags about being <u>your</u> best friend…just the same way you brag about being <u>their</u> best friend?)

Treat yourself like your best friend treats you this week…this month…this year. From now on.

You'll be glad you did.

A Positive Breathing Exercise

The very act of breathing is positive. (Consider the alternative!)

But the next time you're feeling frustrated, anxious, or overwhelmed, I encourage you to try this breathing exercise. Here's how it works:

On the inhale or "in breath" you say "I am..." and on the exhale or "out breath" you say something positive about yourself.

Try it!

(Breath in) "I am..." (out breath) "very confident."

(Breath in) "I am..." (out breath) "extremely healthy."

(Breath in) "I am..." (out breath) "a positive person."

Inhale: "I am..." exhale: a positive or constructive statement about yourself.

"I am...a great manager." "I am...a fabulous salesperson." "I am...very successful." "I am...a good friend." "I am...a positive example."

Are you with me? Not only will you reduce (or eliminate) your feelings of frustration, anxiety, or being overwhelmed, but you'll feel more positive as a result. (And who can't use that in their life?)

You're Always Right

When you get up in the morning, do you think, "Today is going to be a crummy day"? If so, you're right.

If you think, "Today's going to be a great day", you're also right.

If you think life is unfair? You're right.

If you think life is pretty wonderful? You're right.

If you think you've gotten screwed in life? You're probably right.

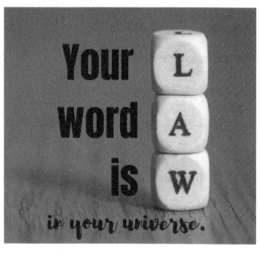

If you think, "This is amazing! What a time and place to be alive – it's unbelievable!" You're right.

Because your word is <u>law</u> in your universe. If you say, "I'm not the kind of person who is successful" - BINGO - then you're not the kind of person who's successful. You just said it! On the other hand, if you say, "I am going to be very successful or will be soon" or "I AM very successful" -- then BINGO! – there is a high likelihood you ARE successful!

Be mindful, be aware of the thoughts you have. Your

word is law in your universe. Once you put it out here and it comes into this dimension, this reality, it becomes REAL.

The more positive things you say, the more positive results you'll have. (Oh, look: I'm right!)

P.S. Keep in mind, sometimes you have to allow a little time for the results you're looking for to appear - not always, because sometimes what you say will happen right away. But other times you may have to wait a bit. Be patient – it's worth it!

> **Whether you think you can, or think you can't, you're right.**
>
> **Henry Ford**

The News and You

Let's talk about the news.

It's become very obvious in recent years that you want to be careful how much news you watch. The news tends to be negative, whether it's on television, on social media, or even on the front page of the newspaper (remember those?)

Be careful. *"Remember, what you ingest, you have to digest."*

One of my students shared her experience with her husband and the news. She told me, "My husband wakes up every morning and watches the news, and he's very negative." She said he was shocked when she told him she wasn't going to watch the news with him any longer. His response? "But how can you give it up, you'll never know what's going on in the world!" She said, "I have a funny feeling I'm going to still know what's going on, because it's out there – it's always out there!"

And she's right. (And she later shared with me how much more positive her outlook is most days!)

Be careful how much news you watch, and be careful how much negativity you let in. Your mind and your heart are sacred places, and you can help keep them that way by adding only the positive things that will enrich your life.

So, be careful of the news!

11. CONNECTION

The All Approach

John Wesley was a British theologian and evangelist of the 1700s who laid the groundwork for today's Methodist church. Wesley said:

> "Do all the good you can.
> By all the means you can.
> In all the ways you can.
> In all the places you can.
> At all the times you can.
> To all the people you can.
> As long as ever you can."
>
> — John Wesley

That quote has been referred to as John Wesley's "Rule of Life"; I'm calling it *The All Approach*.

Powerful stuff and what a great approach to (or rule for) life.

Imagine the world if everyone observed this approach!

Getting Together

Do you have a group of friends who've been in your life forever? Or even just one or two people who you know are always there when you need them? They've got your back.

If you do, you're lucky. Those people are a treasure in your life and you want to make sure and treat them as such. Reach out today and organize a get-together with your friends. Go out to lunch, go play golf, go to dinner, go to a movie, meet and play cards…whatever! Take advantage of every opportunity to gather with those people, have some laughs, toast life, and share your life, your love, your friendship.

When you are at the end of your life, you can look back upon all those times you got together and that's where the good, happy, positive thoughts come from: "Yeah, I had a great life." Don't we all want to be able to say that?

Don't be the person who says "Oh, we need to get together…" and then never acts on it. ORGANIZE IT. Today. This week! Two weeks! It doesn't matter when, it matters if you follow through. If you don't, before you know it, it'll be next week…next month…next year. Just do it: organize a get-together with your friends and have some fun!!!

Great Customer

When you go into a store, are you a great customer?

Remember, when you go into the hardware store, or grocery store, or you're trying on clothes, be mindful of the fact that the people waiting on you have probably been dealing with people all day long…and it's probably a safe bet that some of the people they've had to deal with haven't been very nice.

So, why not try it? Conduct yourself in such a way that when you walk away from them, they say, "She's great!", or "What a great guy!", or "I just love when they come in!"

Be a great customer. Say "please" and "thank you." Don't be demanding or rude. Treat the person helping you exactly as you'd like to be treated yourself. (They ARE helping you, after all!)

Be a great customer and see what happens.

What Goes Around

You've heard the saying, 'what goes around, comes around'.

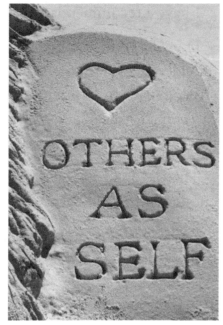

The theory is that whatever goes around comes <u>back</u> around, and it can come back to you tenfold and sometimes even 100-fold! If that's the case, then you'd want to keep your efforts positive, right?

If you want people to understand you, understand them.

If you want people to be considerate of your feelings, be considerate of their feelings.

If you want people to love you, love them.

If you want people to be kind to you, be kind to them.

Another way to say it: "Do unto others as you would have them do until you." It's the "golden rule" concept, and it can be just that simple. And when those positives come back to you tenfold and sometimes even 100-fold, it's a beautiful thing!

It's a great reminder for daily living. Give it a try and see what happens!

Preserve Your Family History

I have a recommendation for you.

Don't let your grandparents, or an older uncle or aunt, or the elders in your tribe leave…pass on…without making the effort to extract information from them. That information can contain valuable history and great wisdom…and you don't know until you ask.

This is done by questioning. Here are some of the questions you could ask:

What was your life like when you were my age?

Did you know your grandparents? What were they like?

Did they ever share stories with you?

What one bit of advice would you give me to make life even better than it already is?

And then listen like your life depends on it. Take notes or just record the session for future reference.

Don't let that wonderful information and wisdom pass by. You're going to find it's a winning proposition for everyone: you'll be surprised to find they might just love talking about it and you'll also be surprised to find how much you love learning about it.

Make the most of the opportunity. Ask those questions.

And have a great time doing so!

Wise Expectations

There's an old man sitting on his front porch of his home on the edge of town. A man pulls up with his family and says, "I am moving to this town, can you tell me what the people are like?"

The old man says, "Well, what are the people like in the town you just came from?"

The man says, "Oh, they're negative, critical, not very good." The old man responds "Well, you will find the people here are about the same."

About a week later, another man pulls up to the old man and asks the same question: "Sir, what are the people like in this town? My family and I are planning to move here." The old man responds, "Well, what are the people like in the town you just came from?"

The man replies, "Oh, they were wonderful! Very kind and giving, helpful, neighborly, wonderful people and a wonderful town!" The old man responds, "Well, you'll probably find the same in this town."

About six months later, the old man is at an event in the town and sees both men. He asks the first one, "So, what's it been like for you here?" The man's response: "You were right: the people are negative and critical, just unbelievable!"

The old man then sees the second man and asks him the same question. He says, "You were absolutely right – they're friendly, they're neighborly, and we love this town!"

The old man knew an important fact: you must remember that your own expectations are not necessarily based in reality; you'll see what you want, or expect, to see. You won't necessarily see what is actually in front of you.

Make sure you set wise expectations!

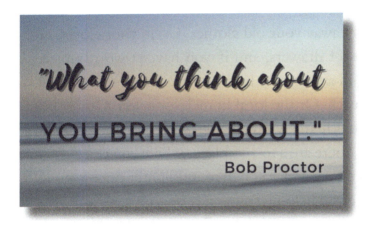

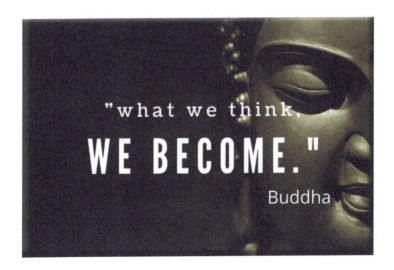

Make A Difference

We all want some pretty simple things out of life: we want to be happy, we want to feel satisfied, and we want to know that our lives make a difference. Those can all mean very different things to each person, so how do you achieve them?

There are three simple actions I recommend.

First: Give away your old clothes. Go in your closet, go to your dresser drawers, and if you haven't worn a piece of clothing in a year, give it away. Give it to the Goodwill. Or your church. Or the local homeless shelter. Or a sober living house. Or the Vietnam Veterans of America. You get the idea: there are a ton of places where you can donate and I guarantee you'll feel better and lighter once you do. Not only are you helping someone else, you're clearing out clutter from your own life.

Second: Give blood. Blood banks are experiencing more shortages than ever. So, if there's a blood drive in your neighborhood, at your local Red Cross, or blood bank, or local library, or the local school, give a pint of blood. It's easy to do, it's painless, and it's something you can do 3-4 times each year (every eight weeks actually) that will help someone who needs it most.

Third: Money may be tight, but there's no time like the present: give money to your favorite charity. My own favorites are the Wounded Warrior Project, Special Olympics, and Doctors Without Borders. I feel really good when I give money to those organizations: I believe in their missions and objectives, and it's a great feeling when I'm able to support them!

Those are just three things you can do to make a difference. Try any one – or all three – and see what happens. It's a safe bet: you're going to feel happy; you're going to feel satisfied, and you're going to know you've made a difference.

Wait and see!

<u>Acknowledgements</u>

I would like to recognize those folks who taught me the life lessons and insights I've been fortunate enough to share in this book. Gratitude goes out to: Ole Larsen; Luis Cordoba; Susan McBride; Katie Beck; Kathy Cheevers; My Father, Richard Beck; My Mother, Louise Beck; Ram Dass; Elizabeth Gilbert; Joseph Chilton Pearce; Stu and the Boys; Dave Knezz; Jeff and Val Gee; my wife Kim Beck and my kids, Richard, Katie and Stephanie; Emily Petroff; and a big THANK YOU to Karen Fouts who 'kept after it'. I wouldn't have been able to complete this book without her.

Made in the USA
Monee, IL
08 August 2024